WORK IT, GIRL

MICHELLE
OBAMA

WORK IT, GIRL

BECOME A LEADER LIKE MICHELLE OBAMA

Written by Caroline Moss

Illustrated by Sinem Erkas

Frances Lincoln
Children's Books

Chapter 1

Happy Birthday, Michelle!

· · · · · · · · · · ·

Michelle LaVaughn Robinson's eyes fluttered open on the morning of January 17th. She had been counting down the days to turning eight years old for what seemed like a really, really long time, and it was finally here!

> SHE JUMPED OUT OF BED, SO EXCITED TO LOOK IN THE MIRROR AND SEE IF SHE LOOKED ANY DIFFERENT TO THE DAY BEFORE.

She examined her face very thoroughly, like a detective on the case, and determined that yes, she definitely did look older than she did just 24 hours earlier, when she was only seven years old. Like she used to do every day, Michelle arranged her stuffed animals around her bed. They all seemed to be smiling at her. She studied her Barbie dolls. They were all impeccably dressed and groomed. As a child, Michelle cared very much about her few personal possessions. Her dolls were her friends.

Michelle could hear voices coming from the rest of the house, so she threw on her school clothes, brushed her teeth and dragged out her big winter coat (it was January in Chicago, after all!) to go and greet her family. Michelle lived with a lot of people. There was her mum, Marian, her dad, Fraser, and her older brother, Craig. They shared a tiny space in the upstairs of a small bungalow-style house with other relatives, who lived in the downstairs part of the house. Sometimes it felt really crowded because it was hard to get privacy. But on days like her birthday, she was grateful to be so close to her family, whom she loved so much. There was always someone else around, and someone to talk to.

"Where's Aunt Robbie?" Michelle said breathlessly, as her mother handed her a piece of buttered toast with scrambled eggs.

"Well Happy Birthday to you, too, Miss Michelle!" Marian Robinson laughed, giving her daughter a big smooch on the forehead, which Michelle promptly wiped off with her forearm. Her eyes darted around the room, looking and listening for signs of Aunt Robbie.

"Is there a birthday girl here?" There she was, Michelle's favourite aunt,

wearing her eyeglasses on a chain around her neck like a big glamorous necklace and singing the 'Happy Birthday' song like it was an operetta. Aunt Robbie was a talented pianist and opera singer and sometimes taught Michelle lessons. She was a little scary, but only because she was so serious and important. Michelle was not scared of Aunt Robbie, but when Aunt Robbie was around Michelle knew she was in the presence of a Very Big Deal.

"It's me! It's me!" Michelle exclaimed. Aunt Robbie smiled at her niece, then walked into her area of the house where her beloved piano sat.

"Can I play piano today?" Michelle peeked her head in and asked Aunt Robbie. "Since it's my eighth birthday?"

"May I play piano today," Aunt Robbie corrected her, and scooted over on the piano stool to make room.

Michelle stared at the keys, suddenly unsure of where to start. She felt her palms begin to sweat. Was it too late to change her mind? Then, Aunt Robbie wordlessly leaned over her and tapped the key right in the middle of them all – the Middle C. Michelle began to play a song.

Michelle was never destined to become a pianist, but her family values and sense of community were built in her hometown of Chicago. These values would inspire her to go on and change communities across the US – and beyond.

"THE ONLY LIMIT TO THE HEIGHT OF YOUR ACHIEVEMENTS IS THE REACH OF YOUR DREAMS AND YOUR WILLINGNESS TO WORK HARD FOR THEM."

— Michelle Obama

Chapter 2

A Very Smart Student

• • • • • • • • • •

Michelle loved two things an awful lot. She loved going to school, and she loved her dad. Well, she loved her whole family, of course, but she really loved her dad, Fraser. Her dad was her hero. Even though he had been diagnosed with a disease called Multiple Sclerosis, or MS (a condition that affects your brain and spinal cord, which causes things like muscle weakness and tiredness), it never seemed like he was slowing down. He even drove a really cool car!

He was always saying something wise, and Michelle learned early on that she should listen very carefully to what her dad would tell her. He seemed to always know best.

And then there was school. Michelle loved school. She loved reading, making up stories in her head and on the page, and creating art.

SHE HAD A BIG IMAGINATION AND SHE TRIED TO EXHAUST IT EVERY SINGLE DAY. SHE LOVED SPELLING TESTS, MATHS TESTS AND SCIENCE PROJECTS.

But this wasn't always the case with the children in her class. And, at eight years old, Michelle's school class was full of other eight-year-olds who always seemed to be bouncing off the walls. This frustrated Michelle to no end. She wanted to learn! She wanted to read books and be quizzed on the passages that she read. But to be excited about school was seen as kind of uncool by her peers, and she didn't exactly make tons of friends.

It didn't bother Michelle that she couldn't find children her own age to connect with. She kept herself busy with her studies, her family and piano lessons with Aunt Robbie. But her teacher was starting to notice Michelle wasn't challenged enough by her schoolwork, and moved her up a class. That was cool! Michelle was proud of herself.

By the time Michelle was about to go to secondary school, she was more aware of the world around her.

She knew her family was not as rich as some of the other children she had grown up with. They didn't have tons of extra money or a big fancy house, even though Michelle would say she didn't go without anything. But money and possessions are important to some, and

their lack of the finer things in life caused small-minded people to look down on Michelle and her family. Plus, being Black – even in Chicago, where there were lots of people from lots of different backgrounds – could be dangerous. When they were younger, Craig was given a brand new bike for his birthday, but a police officer accused him of stealing it. Michelle's mother was so mad that she yelled at the officer and made him apologise to her son. Michelle saw that her mother was strong, and she wanted to be strong, too. Michelle saw her mother's example of demanding respect, and learned a very big lesson that day.

While Michelle was studying hard in secondary school, she started to dream about the kind of university she wanted to go to. Education was the most important thing to Michelle's mum and dad. They didn't get the opportunity themselves, and so they instilled the idea of higher learning into their children. Sometimes they would pile into Michelle's dad's beloved Buick car and drive around the streets with the big houses and the rich, lush gardens. "This is what life could look like if you go to a good university and get a good job," her parents would say.

Craig went to university first, and he chose Princeton University. Michelle wanted to go to Princeton, too. She had worked so hard. She studied constantly, did all of her homework and passed nearly all of her exams (no one is perfect!). So, she was excited to walk into a university advisor's office to tell of her dreams to be a Princeton student. She had never met

this woman before, but it was her job to help students figure out where to apply for university and how to make sure their applications were correctly submitted.

Michelle would never forget the words that came out of the advisor's mouth.

"I'M NOT SURE," SHE SAID, "THAT YOU'RE PRINCETON MATERIAL."

That was a kick in the stomach. If you've ever been told you couldn't be someone or something, you know how Michelle was feeling that day. First it makes you really mad, and then it makes you really sad. What if these naysayers are right? What if they know you better than you know yourself and you really can't do or be who or what you want to be?

Michelle had to think fast. She had spent her whole life preparing to go to university and this advisor didn't know her from Eve. Who was she to say what Michelle could or could not do? Michelle smiled politely, then marched over to Mr. Smith – her neighbour and the assistant principal. Mr. Smith knew Michelle very well, and so Michelle asked him to write her a letter of recommendation to Princeton. He did not bat an eyelid. He wrote her a letter. Michelle took that letter and submitted it, along with her exam results and essays, to Princeton.

Seven months later, she found out she was accepted. What would have happened if she had listened to that university advisor? Would it have changed her path forever?

"I NEVER
MISSED CLASS.

I LOVED
GETTING A'S,

I LIKED
BEING SMART.

I LIKED BEING
ON TIME.

I THOUGHT BEING SMART WAS COOLER THAN ANYTHING IN THE WORLD."

— Michelle Obama

Chapter 3

Princeton

· · · · · · · · · · ·

As Michelle pulled in front of what would be her first-year student house, she felt overwhelmed. Princeton was huge. There were so many people. There were so many trees! She saw boys joking around and laughing like they had known each other for years. She saw first-years looking timid, standing by their parents' cars, waiting to unload cardboard boxes of bedsheets and winter jackets and notebooks.

Michelle's dad had driven her to drop her off. Even though it was hard for him to walk at that point, he stood tall watching his youngest child move into her student house. Fraser Robinson was so proud of Michelle. He was proud of her past and proud of her future.

Princeton was a wildly different world to the South Side of Chicago. Most of the students Michelle saw in lectures, or in the houses or cafeteria, were white. Black students were few and far between.

> **MICHELLE SAID THAT SHE AND HER FELLOW BLACK PEERS 'STUCK OUT LIKE POPPY SEEDS IN A BOWL OF RICE'.**

She had her brother, Craig, who was a little older than she was at Princeton, and her new best friend, Suzanne Alele. Suzanne was a bright ray of sun for Michelle. She was carefree and self-assured. Michelle admired those qualities in her friend and wanted people to see those qualities in her, too. Being around a person like Suzanne helped Michelle bring out the best in herself.

Michelle even had a work-study job, which students on financial aid were required to have to help pay their tuition costs. She worked in a student office, helping people. And she had a cool boss, Czerny, who was about ten years older than Michelle and always asked her great questions. They all started with these three words: "Have you ever...?" Those questions always got Michelle thinking. They helped her think about a world outside of her own.

Even though Michelle met lots of different types of people at university and was exposed to many different ways of thinking and ideas, she still felt like she hadn't seen much of the world. On a trip to New York City with Czerny, she was pushed outside of her comfort zone when Czerny asked her to drive her car a few

times around the crazy New York City streets – because there were no parking spots and Czerny had to run something inside one of the big, tall buildings. Michelle thought, *I can't do that!* But there was no one else who could, and so Michelle was forced to believe in herself, and her ability to drive that car around those city streets. And she did.

It may seem small to you or me, but this was a big turning point. Michelle realised she did not have to blend into the background. She did not always have to take the easy route. She started to imagine herself as a helper and an influential voice in her community, as a smart mind with ideas to share with the world.

As Michelle continued to spread her wings and fly, she would often call home and relay her exciting Princeton stories to her parents. She told them about working at the Fields Center (then named the 'Third World Center'), a support system for students of colour. She loved that job, and her parents were so proud of Michelle: she was the butterfly they always knew her to be. But as Michelle was stepping into her life, her father Fraser's life was slowing down. The disease was getting the best of him, and even though her mum and dad put on brave faces, Michelle knew her father was slowly slipping away from her. She was experiencing so many different emotions at the same time. This was, Michelle realised, 'growing up'.

Chapter 4

When Someone Says You Can't: Prove Them Wrong!

. . . .

It was almost as if Michelle blinked and university was over. Princeton was an amazing place for Michelle. It was a place of personal and academic learning and growth. It was a place of friendship and heartbreak and laughter and tears and late-night studying sessions and even a few parties here and there. It was fun... and now it was over. It seemed like it was only yesterday that Michelle and her dad pulled up to the kerb of her student house and looked nervously around at all of the new sights. Now, Michelle called Princeton home. She knew all the shortcuts and secret study locations, the names of the library staff and how to get from one building to another without a map.

Before she was truly a graduate, her last task would be to write her dissertation, which is like having a really big essay due for homework – but you have a whole year to work on it. Michelle, though a pretty good student, was finding herself distracted near the end of university. She was losing steam, and her lecturers were starting to notice her slipping. They worried about her application to Harvard Law School being rejected.

"You know, you're a good student," her lecturer told her. "But are you the best I've ever seen? I'm not sure."

Do you remember the advisor who doubted Michelle was Princeton material? Well, now she had someone doubting her ability to get into Harvard Law School. If there's one thing we have learned about Michelle LaVaughn Robinson so far it is that when someone says she can't do something, she does everything she can to prove them wrong.

How do you think this story ends? Do you think she got into Harvard Law School? If you answered 'yes', you were right!

> **"EDUCATION WAS TRULY EVERYTHING FOR ME. NEITHER OF MY PARENTS HAD A CHANCE TO ATTEND UNIVERSITY, AND GETTING MY DEGREE CHANGED THE COURSE OF MY LIFE,"** MICHELLE LATER SAID ABOUT GOING TO UNIVERSITY.

> **"THE LESSON I LEARNED FROM THAT IS THAT AS WOMEN AND GIRLS, WE HAVE TO CONFRONT THOSE NEGATIVE VOICES — THE ONES IN OUR HEAD AND THE ONES FROM PEOPLE IN OUR LIVES — TELLING US WHAT WE CAN'T DO,"**
>
> **MICHELLE SAID IN AN INTERVIEW IN 2018.**

Michelle's lecturers and advisors remember seeing a huge difference between the timid first-year and the Princeton graduate, Harvard Law-bound Michelle Robinson. They said she had gained a certain confidence during her time at the university, and recall her work advocating for more Black faculties to better represent the changing makeup of the school. She was destined for big things, and her educators hoped they would someday see her change not just her community, but the world.

If only they knew...

Chapter 5

Before The Rainbow, There Is Rain

· · · · · · · · · ·

When Michelle graduated from Harvard, it was 1988 and she was ready to take the world by storm. She got a job at a law firm called Sidley Austin LLP, where she was only one of a handful of Black lawyers, and she was busy working and learning about her new career. She also had important family issues on her mind – Aunt Robbie had passed away, her father's health was declining and Suzanne, her best friend from Princeton, had been diagnosed with cancer. It was a lot for a recent graduate to handle, and it was hard to deal with.

When you are sad, it's important to take care of yourself first before trying to help others. That will make your efforts easier. But Michelle was a people pleaser.

It was important for Michelle not to be perceived as weak or childlike.

> **SHE WANTED EVERYONE TO THINK SHE HAD IT ALL TOGETHER, EVEN IF IT MEANT BURNING OUT INSIDE.**

All she wanted was for her loved ones to see she was an adult with absolutely no problems. Is that realistic? Have you ever wanted people to view you that way? Or maybe you know someone like this.

Michelle had a lot to juggle, but she was becoming very good at taking on lots of different tasks with a smile. She loved her job, where she was in charge of looking at scripts for TV shows like *Barney and Friends* with her sharp legal eye. She worked really hard, sometimes clocking 60 or more hours a week, and often ate multiple meals a day at the office. She had moved into the downstairs flat of her parents' new house, which was Aunt Robbie's old house. Michelle called it 'a bird in the hand', which meant that she was given an opportunity she would have been silly to feel 'too proud' to take. So she saw her parents whenever she wasn't at the office, which was nice for Michelle; she wanted to spend a lot of time with her father.

She was in a bit of a routine, and that was comfortable for Michelle. Work made her feel grounded and stable, even during the rocky parts of life.

"JUST TRY NEW THINGS.
DON'T BE AFRAID."

"STEP OUT OF YOUR
COMFORT ZONE
AND SOAR..."

— Michelle Obama

Chapter 6

Hi, I'm Barack!

· · · · · · · · · · ·

After being employed at Sidley Austin for a while, Michelle was told a new person would be starting at the firm soon, and she would be tasked with showing him around. His name was Barack Obama... maybe that name sounds familiar to you? At the time, that name did not mean anything, especially to Michelle, who was too busy with work to pay attention to much else.

Michelle was going to be Barack's advisor, which meant she was like his office buddy. She would make sure he was happy at work and that he had all of the resources he needed to get the job done. They also went to fancy lunches, which was a perk of working at a law firm (the company paid!). Barack was touted as a *wunderkind* of sorts, but Michelle was unimpressed in the beginning – he was late to work on his first day.

After a while, Michelle started feeling like Barack was her best friend at work. Michelle remembers how he would always lounge on the sofa in her office to have a chat. They had a lot in common, and Barack was the first person she met at Sidley who really understood the South Side of Chicago. He knew home like she knew home. That brought them together.

"Our pull towards each other was very evident and easy to understand," Michelle would later write in her book, *Becoming*. But she thought it wouldn't look good to date a colleague, so she tucked away her tiny, blooming crush on Barack and focused on her job.

That wasn't hard, as Michelle was still far too busy for dates. It did not even register on her radar that Barack was an eligible bachelor-type, and that it would be a good idea to date him. One day, he asked her out with a big smile on his face. Michelle was taken by surprise and quickly declined the invitation, though she knew she had started to develop a little crush on Barack. But they worked together! However, weeks later, the firm had tickets for two people to see *Les Miserables*... and Michelle decided to invite Barack to go with her, purely on an advisor-advisee relationship (or so she said!)

Turns out, they both hated the show and bailed on their seats during the intermission to get a drink, where they talked and laughed. Michelle dropped Barack off at his house later, where he asked if they could keep 'hanging out' over ice cream – there was a Baskin-Robbins down the street from his flat.

Michelle ordered the chocolate cone, and when Barack asked her if he could give her a kiss, she instantly leaned in to kiss him.

A plaque now sits on the kerb where the couple enjoyed their treats. It has a quote from Barack Obama's book, O: "On our first date, I treated her to the finest ice cream Baskin-Robbins had to offer, our dinner table doubling as the kerb. I kissed her, and it tasted like chocolate."

The next few years were a whirlwind for Michelle. Her relationship with Barack grew serious; she had purchased a journal and began taking notes of her thoughts and feelings, and writing her own story proved to be a helpful way to plot her own roadmap through life. She and Barack exchanged letters when he returned to law school.

Michelle had also experienced a huge loss. Her best friend, Suzanne, had died from cancer. She was so young, and it stunned Michelle. Then more crushing news: at home, Michelle's dad was reaching the end of his life. It was so difficult for her to lose Fraser. He was her rock, her lifeline, her ally. When he went into the hospital for the last time, Michelle held her dad's hand.

Later that night, Fraser had a heart attack and died. He was only 55. Even though Michelle, her brother Craig and her mother Marian were expecting this, it was still such a crushing blow to their family unit.

"I LOVE YOU WITH MY WHOLE HEART, MICH," HE SAID, BARELY ABLE TO GET THE WORDS OUT BECAUSE HE WAS SO SICK. "AND I AM PROUD OF THE WOMAN YOU HAVE BECOME."

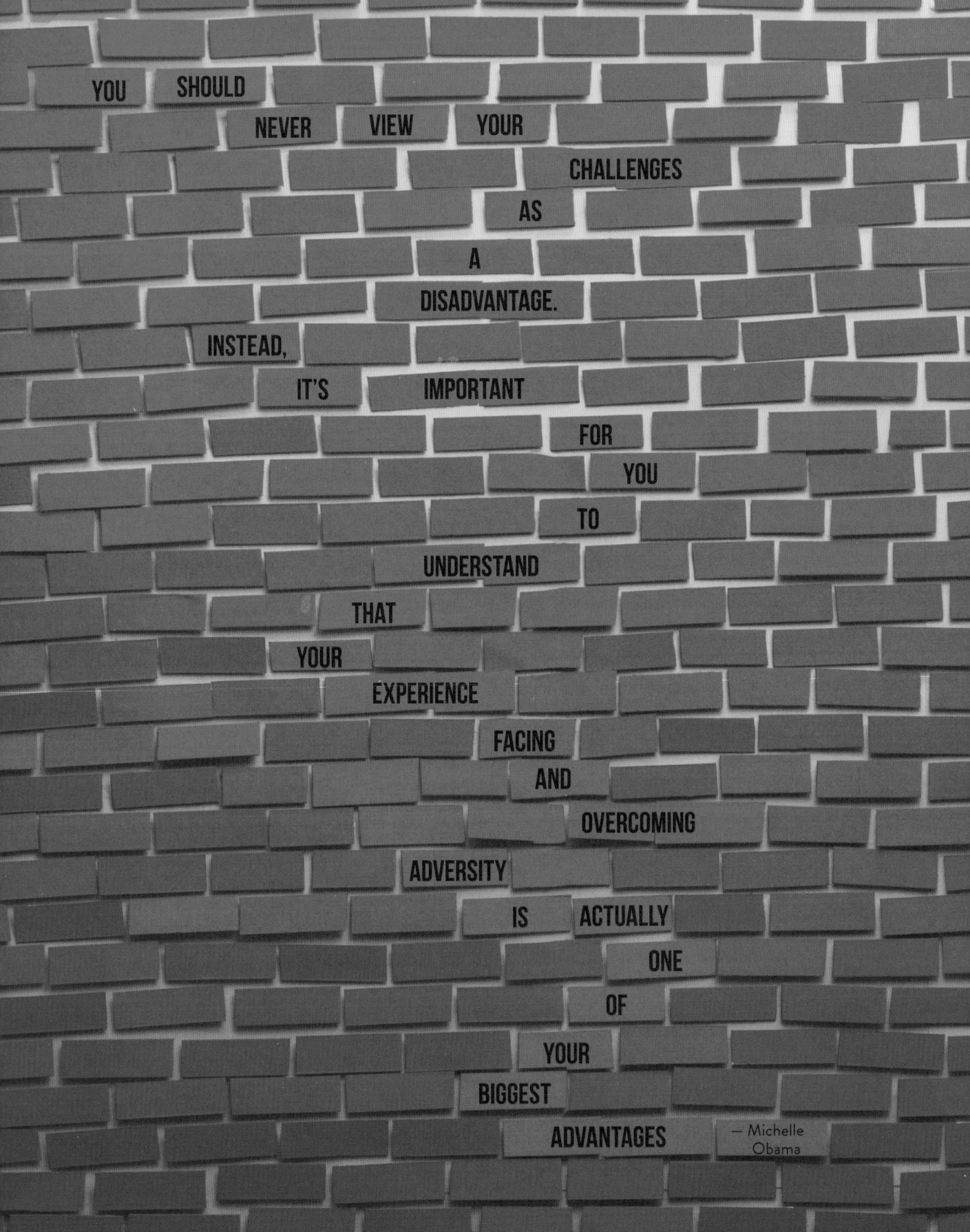

YOU SHOULD NEVER VIEW YOUR CHALLENGES AS A DISADVANTAGE. INSTEAD, IT'S IMPORTANT FOR YOU TO UNDERSTAND THAT YOUR EXPERIENCE FACING AND OVERCOMING ADVERSITY IS ACTUALLY ONE OF YOUR BIGGEST ADVANTAGES

— Michelle Obama

Chapter 7

Who Is Michelle?
Only She Can Decide That

After her dad died, Michelle started to do a lot of thinking. She thought about growing up, and how much she loved school and reading and socialising with her friends. She thought about Princeton and the university advisor who thought she wasn't Princeton material. She thought about the teachers who believed in her and the ones that didn't believe in her, and how it made her work that much harder to prove them wrong. She thought about her job – working 60, 70, 80-hour weeks – and how she happily ate limp, dry salads at her desk because she loved the work.

Her father was gone after 55 short years. If Michelle only lived to be 55, would she look back on her life proudly?

She decided, full-stop, that she didn't want to be a lawyer. But what did she want to be; *who* did she want

AND SHE THOUGHT ABOUT HER BOYFRIEND, BARACK, WHO WAS HER BEST FRIEND, CLOSEST CONFIDANT AND BIGGEST CHEERLEADER.

to be? Michelle had no idea, but she knew she wanted to change the world around her and leave it better than she found it. So she started having conversations with people she knew and trusted who were doing their part to change the world, and they would introduce her to people they knew and trusted who were doing their part to change the world. That is how she met Valerie Jarrett, the chief of staff to the Mayor of Chicago. Wow. She was important! Michelle wanted to know her.

As it turned out, Valerie Jarrett wanted to know Michelle, too. She had heard wonderful things from their mutual friend, Susan, and Valerie wanted Michelle to come and work for her at City Hall. It would be a far cry from her job at Sidley but it would be fun, she promised, and she'd get to make a real difference. Michelle was learning that changing the world around her for the better was a driving force inside of her. She was tempted by the offer.

Simultaneously, her boyfriend, Barack, proposed to her. He put a diamond ring on a dessert plate when they were out to dinner. It was a huge surprise!

She was shocked. Her life had seemingly changed overnight, and Michelle was in charge of that change. It felt great. She could feel her father's presence all around her that day. And when she packed up her desk at Sidley to depart for her new adventure, she knew he would have been very proud of her.

Her first year in the Mayor's office was incredibly busy. She was working a lot, and spending a lot of time around Chicago, seeing new things and meeting new people. Even though she had grown up in Chicago, she realised there was a lot she didn't know about the city. Her job was as busy as before – but it was rewarding, too, because she was directly impacting her community. This helped Michelle to truly thrive. It was fulfilling. Michelle wasn't the only person who noticed that she was excelling. People around her could see it! She was spotted and hired to be the executive director of an organisation called Public Allies.

Public Allies combined all of Michelle's interests neatly into one job. It was perfect. The organisation found inspiring young people who showed promise in making a difference. They were mentored and guided through what the programme called 'apprenticeships' – like short-term jobs where you shadow someone who has been doing the work for a long time. Ideally, these people would then graduate to take leadership jobs inside their communities, and a new generation of activists and leaders in Chicago would be born. Michelle took her job very seriously. After all, it was Chicago who raised her. She may have travelled to Princeton and to Harvard for her education, but she believed in bringing that knowledge home with her.

Michelle's favourite part of the job was finding the allies themselves. You might think that in order to find these allies, Michelle would go to the top schools in the city, or to the richest and most privileged families. Not so!

> **MICHELLE AND HER NEW HUSBAND, BARACK, BELIEVED IT WAS VERY IMPORTANT TO SELECT PEOPLE ON THEIR POTENTIAL, AND NOT ON WHETHER THEY WERE WEALTHY OR LUCKY ENOUGH TO AFFORD TO ATTEND UNIVERSITY.**

She understood that there was a system in place rigged against those who did not have enough money to get ahead in life, and that there was brilliance to be found even when there was not money to be found. This was really the apex of what Michelle believed. Potential could not be bought or sold.

While Michelle thrived at Public Allies, Barack too left Sidley Austin to pursue a noble cause – Project Vote — which helped sign up first-time voters to participate in their local and national elections. Barack helped register 115,000 voters in 1992 when Bill Clinton won the presidential election.

The Obamas were busy, and they were tired, but they were happy. Michelle would later say her chosen career 'could drain you while at the same time giving you everything you'll ever need'. Michelle felt she had truly found her calling. She was exactly where she wanted – and needed – to be. And it felt good.

"Don't ever underestimate the importance you can have because history has shown us that courage can be contagious and hope can take on a life of its own."

> **"SUCCESS ISN'T ABOUT HOW MUCH MONEY YOU MAKE, BUT THE DIFFERENCE YOU MAKE IN PEOPLE'S LIVES."**
>
> — Michelle Obama

Chapter 8
You Want To Run For What?!

· · · · · · · · ·

When you love what you do, time tends to move really quickly. The days turned into weeks, the weeks into months, the months into years. Soon, Michelle had spent three years at Public Allies. She wasn't looking for a new opportunity, but one popped up out of nowhere. The University of Chicago had heard about a young woman named Michelle Obama who excelled at cultivating community and strengthening the core of the city, and they wanted to hire her to do something similar at the university. The University of Chicago was hoping Michelle could create a sustainable programme that would help connect the university with its community. She thought the opportunity sounded amazing and jumped at the chance. Michelle knew it would help her to grow, and take the skills she learned at Public Allies and apply them elsewhere.

Barack, on the other hand, had also done some growing and changing. He was very busy, but he and Michelle prioritised family first. It wasn't always easy, but they made it work. They both worked long hours, but like we talked about, the work was rewarding.

HAVE YOU EVER HEARD SOMEONE SAY, "DO WHAT YOU LOVE AND YOU'LL NEVER WORK A DAY IN YOUR LIFE?" THIS IS HOW BARACK AND MICHELLE BOTH FELT ABOUT THEIR JOBS.

In 1996, the Obamas welcomed their first daughter, Malia. And then in 2001, Sasha joined their family. They were complete. Busy and exhausted, but full of love!

Barack had decided to run for office in the US Senate, which was a huge undertaking, but one that he was really meant for. Like Michelle, he loved public service, and that is what a government job is at its core. It exists to give the people a voice. Barack Obama wanted to be the person who represented the state of Illinois in the Senate. Michelle was wary of the kind of notoriety that would come with being the wife of a state politician. She was not used to doing her work in such an open way. She was also, unlike her husband, wary of politics itself. She knew that public servants didn't always serve the

public the way the role required them to do. She knew that some politicians were motivated by power, money and control. Michelle believed in her heart that her husband's intentions were different, and that ultimately she could not stand in the way of his dreams, because he would never stand in the way of hers. But they made a deal: if Barack lost the election, he would move on from politics altogether and get 'a different sort of job' – as she wrote in her book, *Becoming*. Barack agreed with this deal.

As it turned out, lots of people in Illinois wanted Barack Obama to represent them! He won the election! It was exciting, but it was scary, too. Michelle was nervous that her husband would be too busy to spend time with her and her daughters. Michelle was also busy with her work and dreams. But at the time, it was as if her career took a backseat to her husband's. This made her slightly uncomfortable, though she knew it was an important part of a partnership. In the end, it was a good decision for the Obama family. Though Michelle didn't love politics, she did love having a platform to help make her city and state a better place.

Everywhere she went, people wanted to know if her husband was going to run for president.

AT FIRST MICHELLE WOULD LAUGH. PRESIDENT! HOW CRAZY. BUT THEN SHE BEGAN TO WONDER, WAS IT REALLY THAT CRAZY?

Barack Obama, Michelle's husband, decided to run for president. He was young, inexperienced (all considering!) and Black. There had never been a Black president before. Michelle feared that even though the world had come so far, many people may not have been ready for a Black president. She knew those people were wrong for judging a person by the colour of their skin, but she was also realistic – she knew racism crept into every aspect of living and that while some people had evolved to understand a person with darker skin was no different than a person with lighter skin, stereotypes were hard to get rid of and minds were hard to change. Michelle had to always be aware

that she was likely to be treated differently because of what she looked like. She knew that as a Black woman she had fewer chances to "get it right" than someone with white skin did. She hated how unfair that was. Why put their family, their two small girls, in such a public position?

Ultimately, it came down to Michelle and Barack's shared beliefs. They knew that one person could make a difference – that one person could inspire someone else to make a difference. Isn't that what being a president is all about? Encouraging the nation to make the world a better place for future generations?

Michelle was still a little uneasy about the whole thing, mostly because they had two young daughters who needed stability and routine, and running for office would mean a lot of change in a short amount of time. But ultimately, they made the decision as partners: Barack would run for president.

One of the most important things for Michelle to do during this time was to be herself. She had a story to tell.

And she chose to share that story with the world.

A STORY ABOUT HER SMALL HOUSE IN CHICAGO, STUFFED TO THE BRIM WITH HER FAMILY, ABOUT HER AUNT ROBBIE AND THE PIANO KEYS, ABOUT HER FATHER, ABOUT WHAT IT WAS LIKE TO WORK HARD AND STILL FEEL OUT OF PLACE AT A PLACE LIKE PRINCETON, TO BE TOLD SHE MIGHT NOT BE GOOD ENOUGH.

SOON, EVERYONE WAS TALKING ABOUT MICHELLE OBAMA...

Chapter 9

This First Lady Has A Name

• • • • • • • • • • •

You probably know what happened next, right? Barack Obama became president! Everyone was surprised, including Michelle. Remember, she thought that he probably would not win. It occurred to her that she was being the same as that university advisor had been: doubtful! She was proven wrong.

But something was happening Michelle didn't quite like. She was Michelle Obama, but to the world she kept being introduced as the First Lady or 'Barack Obama's Harvard-educated wife'. Even though she knew this was all part of how politics and media worked, it did sting a bit. She was her own person! She was Michelle, not 'Barack's Wife'. But her husband never treated her like she was less important than he was. So, she chose to ignore the media and those who did not know her, and focus on her family and those who lifted her up and knew her heart.

As a newly public figure, this was a tactic that helped immensely while trying to adjust to life as a 'celebrity'.

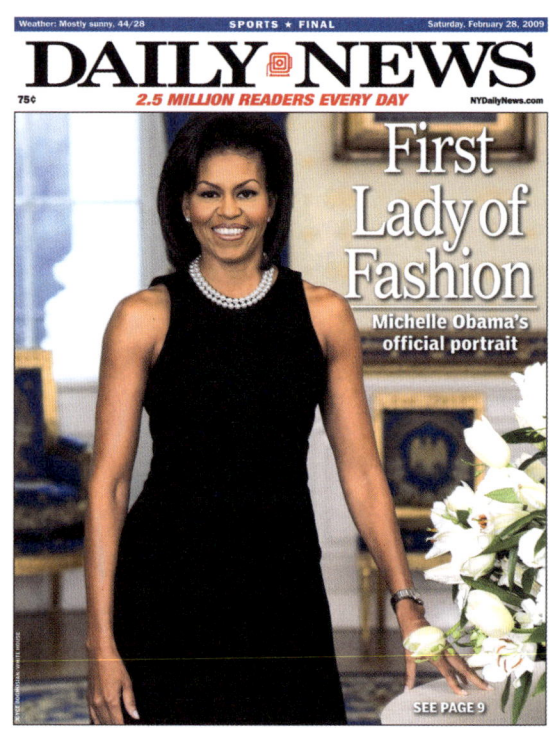

> "WHEN I HEAR ABOUT NEGATIVE AND FALSE ATTACKS, I REALLY DON'T INVEST ANY ENERGY IN THEM, BECAUSE I KNOW WHO I AM."
> —Michelle Obama

Life in The White House was very busy. Not just for Barack, but for Michelle and Malia and Sasha, too. Michelle was tasked with coming up with the ways she wanted to help the country in her now very public position. She thought about all the ways she was helped as a child and all of those in her life who had helped her – like Aunt Robbie, her father, Suzanne from Princeton and her teachers; even the people who had helped her but probably didn't realise they had helped her, like the university advisor who doubted she was Princeton material. If you're wondering how that person helped her, consider this: people who doubt you can often be great motivators for you to do your best work! That's how it manifested for Michelle, and looking back on her earlier years in school, that particular interaction made her incredibly grateful.

Children were very important to Michelle. She believed they were the key to a brighter, stronger, prouder future. Michelle thought long and hard about the ways she could help improve the lives of children all over America. Michelle thought, and thought and thought.

She had some ideas, but none of them were any good. But then she had a great idea, one that would help tons of children, no matter where they lived or what they looked like! She wanted children to be their absolute best selves.

WHAT DID A CHILD'S BEST SELF LOOK LIKE? HOW COULD SHE MAKE THAT HAPPEN? HMMM...

After lots of thinking and lots of talking to those she trusted, Michelle came up with her 'official initiative' for her time at The White House. This is a big project that first spouses commit themselves to during the duration of their partner's presidency. Michelle was ready to unveil her big plan, called 'Let's Move!' for children, which helped put into place programmes to keep children healthy through education and by building good habits. Healthy children were ones who fed their bodies yummy food to help them grow; ones that did lots of running around, playing and adventuring to give them energy; and ones that explored all of the good and beautiful things in the world that they could learn to help their minds expand.

Building these healthy, growing habits as children, Michelle knew, would encourage them to grow into successful, ambitious, dreaming adults. She knew that these children – the ones eating vitamin-rich veggies and fruits, and spending time outside of school playing sports or dancing or running around – were the key to a stronger, healthier, better-for-you-and-me America. Michelle was single-mindedly focused on this huge effort, and she was determined to see her dreams through.

One of the biggest, and most important, aspects to Michelle's 'Let's Move' initiative was the importance of community. As you now know, working within communities was Michelle's strong suit growing up, and it's what drew her to all of the jobs she had during and after university. She knew 'Let's Move' would only succeed if it was truly working within the communities and schools that made up the country.

Michelle was not new to this game, which made her a great success at her work.

Chapter 10
The Story Doesn't End Here

• • • • • • • • • • •

Time flies when you're having fun, as the saying goes. Soon Michelle, Barack, Sasha, Malia and their two puppies Sunny and Bo had to pack up and leave the White House. But Michelle knew her story had just begun, though it was so hard to say goodbye to the big house that had become her home.

She had been able to accomplish so much in the eight years she had spent in Washington DC. She had made speeches, got to know fellow Americans and encouraged a whole new generation of children to get up and MOVE! She had become a role model for women not just in America, but all over the world. She was the first African-American First Lady, and she took that position very seriously. Plus, it always seemed like she and Barack had an amazing relationship. It was like they were best friends first, and that they really loved, respected and cared about each other. People could see that when they saw them on television. That was inspiring. Barack knew his wife was his equal. They were good role models for couples and for parents.

Michelle had to think about what she wanted to do after The White House. She thought back to primary school and the time she felt she was outgrowing her

classroom, and how she sought out the opportunity to move up a class to fulfil her potential.

She thought about high school, and the college advisor who we all know doubted her, and how it motivated her to prove that advisor wrong. Michelle thought about Princeton, and the lessons she learned both in the classrooms from valued professors, and outside of the classroom with her friends and colleagues.

She thought about Harvard, and how she did not know that she wanted to be there until she was actually there, and how she truly realised how much she loved to learn and build community there.

She thought about working at Sidley Austin and meeting Barack for the first time. How he was late for his first day and how she would roll his eyes when he'd flirt with her. Then she thought about the ice-cream date and the kisses that tasted like chocolate. How lucky she had been!

Michelle thought about her father, Fraser, who never got to see her change the world from the White House, but how proud he would have been if he had seen her. Michelle thought about her jobs in Chicago, and what it meant to her community to represent people who

looked like her at the highest rank of politics in the country. And she thought about how nervous she had been to jump into this life with Barack and hold this honour. She was happy, in the end, that she had decided it was a good idea.

Michelle looked around the White House hallways that had once looked so unfamiliar but had soon become hallways where she walked with her family, where she tossed tennis balls to Sunny and Bo, and where she did some of her best thinking. She was not ready to say goodbye, but she knew she had to. She thought about what her father might have said to her in this moment: "Do what you say you're going to do, be honest and true." That made Michelle feel calmer. She knew everything was going to be okay; that this would not be the end, but the beginning.

Michelle knew that her story would impact others. That her journey could be understood by women all over the world if she was brave enough to put it into words. She knew there was a great vulnerability in sharing the stories closest to her heart, but that there was great risk in not sharing those stories with others. Sharing her truth is a form of leadership Michelle knew was important.

New adventures awaited for Michelle and her family, and she knew that it would only be a matter of time before she set out to change the world once more.

Become a leader like Michelle!

10 key lessons from Michelle Obama's life

1 **You are allowed to like what you like!** Michelle loved learning, even if her friends didn't consider school to be very cool. She was not ashamed by her love of knowledge.

2 **Not everyone needs to believe in you if you believe in yourself.** Not everyone thought Michelle had what it took to be successful. But Michelle learned to believe in herself. When you believe in yourself it's easier for people to learn to believe in you.

3 **Cherish the relationships you have with those closest to you.** Michelle loved her family and friends. She knew it wasn't about being the most popular but about having people who she could depend on and who could depend on her.

4 **Think about what you love to do, and figure out what kind of a career would support it.** Michelle was community-driven and wanted to find a job that would help her continue to grow. You can turn your passions into careers.

5 **Try different things and move on when they no longer serve you.** Michelle started out as a lawyer at Sidley Austin LLP but knew she was ready to move on when the time was right. You never need to stay in the same place for longer than you want to.

6 **New friends can help you grow!**
Michelle and Barack both learned from each other and grew together. Being open to new friendships and relationships can help nourish the heart and soul.

7 **Don't be afraid to say 'NO' or to be honest about your true feelings.** When her husband wanted to run for public office, Michelle spoke her mind freely because she knew she was safe and empowered to do so (a mark of a good and healthy friendship or relationship). She was not sold on the idea but ended up making an important compromise with her husband – if he were to lose the election, he'd have to move onto something else.

8 **Don't sacrifice who you are to be whoever someone else wants you to be.**
In one of the most visible and public positions in the country, Michelle felt the pressure to succumb to who people wanted her to be. But she knew being herself was the ticket to gaining the trust of the country and to have her message ring loud and clear. She was a true leader in this way.

9 **Stay humble and unchanged by fame, power and money.**
Michelle stayed true to herself throughout her time in The White House. She wanted people to relate to her, and she knew that by revolving her life around what she cared about – community – she would always be able to recognise herself.

10 **Be optimistic. Good energy attracts great things!**
Michelle always lived with the mentality that great things were ahead of her and the best was always yet to come. Every day can be a new adventure!

Grab a sheet of paper & a pencil and answer these questions!

Michelle Obama believed in giving back to her hometown and community. What would you like to do for your hometown if you could?

. . . .

Michelle spoke her mind when Barack said he wanted to run for president. Can you remember a time you have spoken clearly about your feelings? If not, can you think of anything you would like to say to someone close to you?

. . . .

Imagine you want to run for a government position. What are the main things you care about? Make your own campaign leaflet to summarise them. What would you do once you achieved the position?

. . . .

Michelle is a wonderful public speaker. Watch some of her speeches online, or read the quotes from this book, and write or recite your own speech into a mirror.

Further Reading

• • • • • • • • • •

Take a look at these other great books and resources to learn more about Michelle Obama. You can also read about and help the organisations she supports, or has founded, listed below.

Non-fiction
The Extraordinary Life of Michelle Obama by Sheila Kanani and Sarah Walsh
Of Thee I Sing: A Letter to My Daughters by Barack Obama
Young, Gifted and Black by Jamia Wilson and Andrea Pippins
Who Is Michelle Obama? by Megan Stine
Who Is Barack Obama? by Roberta Edwards

Advanced Reading
Becoming by Michelle Obama
Chasing Light: Michelle Obama Through the Lens of a White House Photographer
by Amanda Lucidon
Michelle Obama: Speeches on Life, Love and American Values by Michelle
Obama, and edited by Stacie Vander Pol
Dreams From My Father by Barack Obama

Organisations
Obama Foundation
Girls Opportunity Alliance
My Brother's Keeper Alliance
Reach Higher
Let Girls Learn

Online
Learn the 'Move Your Body' dance routine with Beyoncé on YouTube,
part of Michelle Obama's 'Let's Move! Flash Workout' initiative.

Inspiring | Educating | Creating | Entertaining

Brimming with creative inspiration, how-to projects, and useful information to enrich your everyday life, Quarto Knows is a favourite destination for those pursuing their interests and passions. Visit our site and dig deeper with our books into your area of interest: Quarto Creates, Quarto Cooks, Quarto Homes, Quarto Lives, Quarto Drives, Quarto Explores, Quarto Gifts, or Quarto Kids.

Work It Girl: Michelle Obama © 2020 Quarto Publishing plc.

Text © 2020 Caroline Moss. Illustrations © 2020 Sinem Erkas.

First Published in 2020 by Frances Lincoln Children's Books, an imprint of The Quarto Group. 400 First Avenue North, Suite 400, Minneapolis, MN 55401, USA.T (612) 344-8100 F (612) 344-8692 **www.QuartoKnows.com**

ISBN 978-0-7112-4517-4

The illustrations were created in paper

Set in Brandon Grotesque and Bebas Neue

Published by Katie Cotton

Designed by Sinem Erkas

Paper Modelling by Sinem Erkas and Christopher Noulton

Paper Assistants: Tijen Erkas, Nick Gentry, Lora Hristova

Edited by Katy Flint

Production by Nicolas Zeiffman

Manufactured in Guangdong, China CC112019

9 8 7 6 5 4 3 2 1

Photographic acknowledgements: p42, Obama And Supporters Rally On Night Of New Hampshire Primary © copyright Win McNamee via Getty Images; p48, Daily News front page February 28, 2009, © copyright New York Daily News Archive via Getty Images; p50, Barack Obama Holds Election Night Gathering In Chicago's Grant Park © copyright Scott Olson via Getty Images.